Poems
For The
Harley Rider

Bill Heffron

Poems for the Harley Rider is a work of fiction and not intended to portray any real person or events.

Preface

This collection of poems is dedicated to and mostly derived from all the riders that I have ridden with since I first crossed my leg over a motorcycle in 1964. Many were and are still good friends, some riders I rode with only once and hardly knew their names. Several have ridden to that big poker run in the sky; I remember their spirit and miss them dearly.

I thank all of you for the great rides, side splitting laughter, extraordinary memories and the fodder for this collection of poems!

I would also like to thank the Mahopac writers group, for their tolerance and insight. They corrected my grammar, punctuations and kept me from slaughtering too many literary rules.

Last but certainly of most importance, I would like to thank Harley Davidson Motorcycles Incorporated for building the finest motorcycles in the world over the last one hundred years.

B i l l   Heffron
(The   Senator)

D i s c l a i m e r

I would like to be very clear about my writing. First, there are no hidden references to God, the devil, or covert codes to set off radical actions by any fanatical groups. My poems are just a collection of thoughts from my fertile Harley mindset. Enjoy them for what they are. Enjoy finding double meanings, subtle twists and intertwining playful thoughts. Please try not to read any negative meanings into any one of them.

Second, I am not prejudiced against any ethnic group of people, their products or religions. All the remarks in this collection of poems are for purposes of rhyme and are written with tongue in cheek, humor. We should all be able to laugh at ourselves or each other from time to time without starting a world war!

Third, I haven't done and don't condone or recommend any of the antics that are depicted in any of my poems. I especially refer to the driving of a motorcycle or any motor vehicle under the influence of alcohol or drugs.

Fourth, I would also like to say for Harley Davidson's sake that all references to oil leaks and mechanical failures are written in good sport, again tongue in cheek humor and refer to the older models, now antiques. Harley Davidson Inc. makes the "BEST" Motorcycles in the world and the world is a better place because of them!

Index

1. The First 100 Years
2. 100 For Freedom
3. Harley History
4. Bill's Harley
5. Pig Roast
6. Dead Flies
7. Raffle Winner
8. Perfect Ride
9. Pot Hole
10. The Gallery
11. An Errand
12. Harley Friends
13. Pepper Sprout
14. Horrible Sound Of The Crash
15. Harley Wallet On A Chain
16. The Journey
17. Little Puddle
18. Straight Pipes
19. Harley Brain
20. Push Button Start
21. Rain Riding
22. Drunken Rider
23. Harley Sportster
24. Broken Bones
25. Macho
26. The Escape
27. Ah Shit
28. Harley Big Twin
29. Rules To Fly By
30. Harley Road King
31. Dazed And Confused
32. First Harley Friends
33. Harley Headlight
34. School Bus Smoke
35. Riding Home
36. Gone Fishing
37. Took Delivery
38. Little Oil Leak from Hell
39. Guy With The Bug
40. Lovey Dove & Me
41. Bad Behavior
42. Recipe For Passion
43. 1976 Liberty
44. Emotions
45. Tidd Bits
46. Getting Stroked At 60 MPH
47. Adrenalin Shot
48. There's A Poker Run Today
49. The Repair
50. Costly Repair

51	Girls Like You	76.	We Wheel
52.	The Antique Harley	77.	Biker Promenade
53.	Sportster Gas Tank	78.	Harley Rider Feel So Free
54.	Drifting Off	79.	The Judge
55.	The Ride By	80.	Sweetie Pie & I
56.	Fat Girl	81.	Harley Davidson
57.	Heaven's Gate	82.	Demons
58.	The Slamming Of Second Gear	83.	Harley Four Speed
59.	Ready Set Go	84.	Friendly Ass-holes
60.	Troubles	85.	Birthday Gift
61.	Harley Lullaby	86.	Ride To Work
62.	Tired Old Harley	87.	Harley Rider At Night
63.	Harley Logo Shield And Bar	88.	Sundays Ride
64.	Trashed	89.	Traffic Jam
65.	Bad Tire	90.	Harley Helmet
66.	Butcher Mechanic	91.	Pissed
67.	Bad Spelling	92.	Road Rage Lug Nut
68.	Road Rash	93.	Traffic Fairy
69.	Shots	94.	I Got She Got
70.	Race Time	95.	The Skid Mark
71.	Live Harley	96.	Gear Gremlin Grungy Grinch
72.	Fast Trip	97.	Downpour
73.	Harley Front Wheel	98.	Loose Chain
74.	Satan Spawned	99.	Rumble Withdrawal
75.	The Lesson	100.	Early Morning Ride

The First 100 Years

Your call to arms in 1903
William S. Harley
William A. Davidson
Walter Davidson Sr.
Arthur Davidson Sr.
A vision to build a motorcycle
Now realized beyond all wildest dreams
An idea and a 10x15 wooden shed
Encroaching the railroad tracks
Evolving, morphing into
The lone American survivor and
A leviathan among motorcycle manufactures
One hundred years a legend
As American
As motherhood and apple pie
Loyalty to our nation and your riders
Four men who are motorcycle history
Fathers of the Harley Davidson mystique and
Harley's unique sound that beckons to our soul
Your machines transport us
Like wind through silk
Gliding along intertwining threads
Of yellow striped blacktop
Four American men
Building American motorcycles
For Americans to ride
With orgasmic passion for their
Machines and their country
Harley Davidson founding fathers
For the first 100 years of
Pleasure and service
WE STAND AND SALUTE YOU!!!

1

100 For Freedom

It started as a lark
A few lines on an airliner
San Francisco bound, business trip
A short Harley Davidson poem
Scribbled on a yellow-lined pad
Then revised, and revised again and again
Emotions consumed my core
Poetry, the touching of the soul
Harley riders have souls
Some have no heart, I've heard
But they all have souls
I had to write more, too many tales to be told
The idea for a book
A wallet on a chain poetry book
A dream, 50 my goal, surely a book, from my soul
Worked hard wrote 16, had to shelve all, save one
The breaking of a union, man and woman, lawyers, greed
Starting over, a writers group
Grammar rules and spelling lessons
A new goal: 100 poems to free my soul
Harley Davidson riders earned this toll
Hours, scratch notes, agony and fall down laughter
Countless memories and emotions
Persistence, dedication to task
And time, so much time
All meld to fulfill a dream
My book of Harley Davidson poems
Each one had to say Harley somewhere in the poem
Hope you enjoy my effort and
Hoping to push your start button more than once
With this collection of my Harley Davidson Poems

HARLEY HISTORY

Harley history America's pride
      you are number one
Start one up and you'll be eyed
      by every mother's son

Learn the history why we ride
      loyalty by the ton
Let the knock offs run and hide
      or they will be shunned

Gave armed forces a great ride
      starting with World War 1
Ride with patriots side by side
      proudly into the sun

Harley history America's pride
      you are number one
Moment of silence for riders that died
      when the day is done

Bill's Harley

Steel, paint, wire, rubber and chrome
Air, fuel, spark and combustion
Births
A mechanical life
Into this iron steed
Called
Bill's Harley
Whirling gears, pistons and cams
Propel Bill
For the thrill of the ride
For Harley and American pride

Pig Roast

Pig roast, pig roast you're the best
It's time to darn my Harley vest
I will bring my girlfriend as a guest
Expand my waistline and lust for her chest
Pork and beer add to the fest, so
A full plate completes my quest
I ate all that food now I need to rest, but
I'm still hungry, no; just a jest, now I'm
Heading back home to my nest
Reciting a Harley poem by ~ bill ~
As I'm heading west…

Dead Flies

Dead flies on my vest
       hitting with a splat
Heading back to my nest
       found also on my hat

Fitting end to the pest
       one less we have to scat
Dead flies are the best
       anyone can tell you that

Badge of courage on my chest
       fly lost his combat
More dead flies is my quest
       big juicy and fat

Ride my Harley just for jest
       spoiled like a brat
Heard there's more flies to the west
       aiming for the gnat

Raffle Winner

The man on the bike
that roared
Down in the saddle
he soared

Winning raffle ticket
cash reward
For this Harley he
couldn't afford

Feeling like a king
just adored
Harley riding home
love restored

Slicing wind like
a sword
Man and machine
perfect chord

Perfect   Ride

Gliding along ribbons of endless blacktop
Etched by a yellow line
Warm crystal day
Glorious clear blue sky
Harley propelled
Man holding handlebars
Woman holding man
Emotions excelled
Feelings of harmony and union
Harley, man, woman, and the universe....

Pot-hole

Harley cruising late last June
    enjoying this ride
It appeared just after noon
    cruising with my bride

A pot-hole the size of the moon
    hold on tight I cried
Knocked my spokes out of tune
    big, jagged and wide

Ruined my whole afternoon
    I took it in stride
It came up much too soon
    a Franklin is eyed

My front tire looks like a prune
    cannot be denied
Timing is most inopportune
    my wallet is fried

The Gallery

Sitting in the gallery drinking a beer
Show them
Show them is what you hear
Arrived too late had to sit to the rear
Harley shirt lifted brings on a cheer
Some of these ladies have great gear
Beautiful breasts to my eye brings a tear
Haven't seen this much flesh since last year
If you don't like this you must be queer
Wasn't sitting there long, honest dear

An   Errand

An errand that I can run
      when I find the time
Just before the day is done
      the pleasure will be mine

Harley and me just one on one
      getting there on a dime
This ride will be great fun
      excitement rise and shine

An errand to run for this lucky son
      my Harley gets a prime
I'll be back home soon hon
      following the yellow line

This damn package weighs a ton
      but it's finally mine
All money spent broke as a nun
      happiness bliss divine

Harley   Friends

To my Harley friends one and all
I'll go riding just give a call
We'll drive safely so we don't fall
But give it some gas, man so it don't stall
Light that bone will have a ball
I'm a northern boy but I'll ride with U-all
My little sportster can really haul, but
Passing that cop, took some gall
Back it down now, rider
To avoid hitting that wall

Pepper Sprout

Hotter than a pepper sprout
My Harley's spark is lit
Hear the roar there is no doubt
I got no time to sit

Leathered up I'm stepping out
Exploiting all my grit
Look at me I want to shout
My pride will never quit

US made and very stout
Jap bikers do admit
Harley riders have the clout
Conceit a little bit

Heading down that well worn route
Be there in just a bit
Riding freely all about
My soul I do commit

Horrible Sound Of The Crash

Horrible sound of the crash
Harley and me on our ass
All that gravel creates road rash
And deep in my arm is a gash
Sliding down the road
Turns skin to ash
Wishing I hadn't smoked that hash
Hope the cops don't find my stash
But after time the pain will pass
Hit a UPS truck, but I got no cash

Harley Wallet On A Chain

Harley wallet on a chain
      back and forth you slip
Tethered to me you'll remain
      looking very hip

Money safely to obtain
      secured by a springy clip
Lost wallet I'd go insane
      my mind would take a flip

All new papers to attain
      I could loose my grip
That would surely fry my brain
      it would skip and dip

I should start a new campaign
      It would be a rip
All men's wallets tethered to a chain
      even if you strip

The   Journey

I mount my two-wheeled iron horse
For transportation, one may hear me say
Nay
For transportation, maybe so
But
Truth be known
It's
For the thrill of the journey
For the wind in my face
For the five hundred and eight pounds of steel
Under my command
Yeah
Truth be known
My Harley launches my spirit to a special place
For transportation, may be so
Ah, but how I travel, also travels my spirit
Being brave of heart
I choose to let it soar

Little Puddle

Little puddle on the floor
    you bring out all my fury
Move my Harley out the door
    in its shining glory

Hidden leak is such a bore
    marking territory
Makes me curse just like a whore
    my costly two wheel dory

Little puddle on the floor
    I'll take this to the jury
Please dry up return no more
    you're such a sticky story

One more leak there will be war
    hang you like a Tory
With speedy-dry I hit you four
    you are my territory

Straight   Pipes

Harley straight pipes are so loud
I think I may have to think aloud
Just like Moses splitting the crowd
Speeding past the true bloods bowed
I'll smoke the tire to be wowed
My lit up tire creates a cloud
Harley straight pipes you're so loud
Noise and speed just does me proud

Harley   Brain

You can't see my Harley brain
But it is alive
Ruling wisely it does reign
Helping me survive

Riding knowledge I did gain
Ripened I arrive
Unsafe riding I distain
Safety I contrive

If you could see my Harley brain
You just might connive
To seek the knowledge I contain
Guard it like a hive

Gliding safely in my lane
I won't take a dive
Cautiously avoids the pain
Gospel that's no jive

Push   Button   Start

Push button start saves my knee
Light the fire cause it's time to flee
That Harley rumble I'm full of glee
No paining patella stinging like a bee
No kicking cursing and buddies laughing at me
Or pain in the groin if I have to pee
Conversion to electric start was worth the fee
Nothing good ever comes for free

Rain Riding

Riding along starts to rain
        road's become slick
Trip evolves into a pain
        and it won't be quick

Driving like this is insane
        better timing I couldn't pick
Keep my eye on wet terrain
        my stomach's a little sick

Rain clouds should be slain
        dry road would be the trick
Riding pleasure down the drain
        slowly time did tick

If you've been caught in the rain
        with an unlucky chick
Then I don't have to explain
        each raindrop's like a brick

Drunken   Rider

Drunken rider stupid fool
Didn't use your head
Too much time on the bar stool
Trouble now lies ahead
Riding drunk is not cool
DWI arrest you now dread
Harley and gravity do a duel
Weaving home toward your bed
Drunken rider stupid fool
Just remember what I said
Riding drunk is not cool
You could end up dead

Harley   Sportster

Harley sportster work of art
    your destiny's di-vine
Push the button and hear you start
    thrilled that you are mine

How you sound pumps my heart
    you're sure looking fine
I'm looking for a course to chart
    a shortcut I'll refine

Throttled pegged off like a dart
    tacking the red line
I'm leathered up and looking smart
    putting on the shine

Speeding to the Harley mart
    north on route Nine
Hundred bucks spent for my cart
    my change is a dime

Broken   Bones

Broken bones snap like a twig
Wishing my Harley had time to zig
Crashing straight into that rig, was
Thrown around like an Irish jig
I was going as fast as a Russian Mig
Why'd that truck have to be so big
Thought my grave they'd have to dig, but
Cheated Grim Reaper out of his vig
I'm alive, broken up, but can you dig
Got the speeding ticket from the pig

Macho

Riding my Harley
Surely is my bag
Devoted biker
Truth man that's no gag

Riding X is like
Reading a cheap rag
Harley spirits high
Never let them sag

All us Harley guys
Really like to brag
Being so macho
Makes my lady nag

Type A behavior
Sometimes is a drag
I must hurry but
End up in a lag

The   Escape

The pressures of the job
And
Dealing with realities of everyday life
You know
Wife, children, bills, telemarketers,
Insurance salesman, police, attorneys, judges
Then enters the tax man….
All wanting a piece of you
And You
A big, hairy, tattooed, bubbling caldron of churning testosterone
Fighting back the rage with every ounce of your fiber
Now mounting
Your two wheeled, iron magic carpet, called Harley Davidson
The world as you know it
Is about to be replaced
By a rumble
The big shift
Breath taking acceleration
The wind in your face
And the only decision to make
Should I shift now…
Or wait for the red line
Euphoria!
No drugs or alcohol needed…

Ah   Shit

Ah shit, Ah shit
Well it needs to come apart
Cause my Harley doesn't start
Ah shit, Ah shit
Well I better get the part
Broken sportster breaks my heart
Ah shit, Ah shit
The old lady's gonna fart
When she hears the cost of the part
Ah shit, Ah shit
I just put in the new part
And it still doesn't start
Ah shit, Ah shit

Harley Big Twin

Harley big twin ridden by Werner
      you're a perfect ten
Bikers know he had to earn her
      let me hear Amen

American pride's a bit more sterner
      calling all real men
Ridden by this guy named Werner
      not like Barbie's Ken

Twisted throttle's a back tire burner
      testosterone strikes again
Makes a Jap biker a quick learner
      tach tells Werner when

Speeding Werner mach one yearner
      precision like Big Ben
Rubber blacktop and gear burner
      swiftly to Werner's den

Rules To Fly By

Sometimes us bikers say " Gotta   Fly   "
So
Here are some of the rules to fly by
Or
Not to fly by
As the case may be
Mount Your Harley Davidson
Rule number, One
Never ride faster than your Guardian Angel
Can fly....
Never flinch nor choke;
When you smile and between your teeth
Goes the fly
Never ask the pilot if
He knows how to fly
Never catch your dick
In your fly...
Never take the bus
When you can fly...
Never use your credit card
When you're on the fly....
Never get high
When you're gonna fly....

Harley   Road   King

Harley Road King
A name has never
Been kinder
To a gentle giant
As thee

A majestic leviathan
Readily cruising
Black yellow striped paths
To unknown infinities
Destined only by fortune

Rider sitting up straight
Like a king on his
Thundering throne
Handle bars as wide
As Texas

Smooth as a well oiled
Baby's ass
You
R U L E

Dazed And Confused

I takes my Harley for a wild ride
I have an empty bladder but my gas tank is full
I keep riding but I gain no distance
I'm going fast yet I'm standing still
I'm looking at the sun but it is still dark
I'm heading forward but I'm looking back
I hit the brakes yet I'm gaining speed
I shifted up but the tach red lined
I leaned into the corner but the road was straight
I'm looking down but can't see the road
I'm out of gas but I have a full tank
I'm doing ninety but there is no wind
I turn the handlebars but I'm still going straight
I look at the tach but I see miles per hour
I know where I'm going but I can't find my way
I have my eyes open but I cannot see
I feel my Harley's pulse but it has no flesh
I'm all grown up but acting like a child
I just crashed..... but I'm still riding........

First   Harley   Friends

Louie and Nick my first Harley friends
When we called old Thirty and above
There was not a gray hair
To be found between three heads
Life tugs each of us in different directions
States divide
And we keep riding
Life's curves keep coming
So do the children
But old friendships never die
And we keep riding
Gray hair abundant now
Can't find a brown hair among three heads
We ride a little more cautious now
Haven't done a wheelie down Main Street in over thirty years
Broken bones mend slower over fifty
And we keep riding
Long gone is our Harley youth and spring in our step
Conversations about horsepower, cams and gears
Migrated to topics like back aches from hell
Taking longer to get off the bike once you got there
Than the trip took
Boys' night out to cruise evolved into
Talking about the old boys' nights out
To cruise
 Fond memories of yester year
And we keep riding

Harley   Headlight

Harley headlight shine so bright
　　　lighting up my way
Guide me safely throught the night
　　　home before the day

Leaning through the corner tight
　　　hope the tires stay
If you went out there's instant fright
　　　and hell I'd have to pay

Returning from a party tonight
　　　with a girl named Fay
Owing our life to your light
　　　heading for the hay

You and I've become so tight
　　　she said not today
Trusting you with all my might
　　　the next date I may

School Bus Smoke

Early morning and I'm off to work
My Harley's the chariot of choice today
Fresh air billows into my lungs as I ride
Making me feel so alive and free
Feeling like a part of my machine
Rounding the corner, I'm stopped by
A big yellow box, packed with
Little urchins on their way to school
Little boys peer at me with wonder and awe
Wishing they were me
A smile erupts on my face
Remembering when I was crammed into a box like that
Homework incomplete, heading for a test
Wishing that I was going anywhere but to school
Now today I'm riding free just Harley and me
The bus lurches, black smoke
Belching from its exhaust pipe
Bringing my breathing to an abrupt stop
And reality to a start
I'm on my way to work, short handed
And today, is my IRS audit !

34

Riding Home

Riding my Harley home
Like I always do
Another mile rolled by
Daydreaming of you

Weary from work
I lust for your bod
Coaxing the throttle
On my two wheel hot rod

When united again
We'll rumble in bed
Stroking the hair
On your beautiful head

Twenty miles to go
Soon there'll be bliss
Only moments away
From a passionate kiss

Gone   Fishing

The sun's not yet awake, but I am
A faint golden glow silently announces sunrise
Soon to light the mountains toward East
Quietly I strap my fishing pole to my Harley's handlebars, now
Downloading my ass into the saddle, with a slight tug
My iron steed raises upright, ready for that thumb command
That ignites my Harley's soul;
Not now my eager mechanical wonder it's AM 4:30, you see
Good fences make good neighbors, says they
But no match for your ear splitting straight pipes, says I
Straight pipes and 4:30 the AM, holds
Unwanted early reveille for all neighbors
Patience my chosen one, with a gentle push to the edge of the drive
Down the mountain road we silently glide
Eagerly awaiting that moment, out of earshot
I open your gas valve, twist your key, then
Pop your beastly custom clutch, cranking life into your soul
Anticipating your ear splitting roar, instinctively
 I hang on tight as you sprint to life and launch me onward
To those helpless little fish....

Took   Delivery

I took delivery on my new Harley today
Reality sets in
Sensory satisfaction in overload
All cares gone by the time I hit third gear
The road keeps appearing in my face, as
I accelerate, feeling my new Harley's essence
Getting acquainted
The wind gently squeezes the skin
To my boney face, and whips my beard
Like a willow tree in a hurricane
Notify my next of kin
I may never be seen again
My reptilian brain now firmly in control
Reality is the wind, the power and the rumble
There is no reality, like the machine
I'm riding.......

Little Oil Leak From Hell

Little oil leak from hell
    a drop where you stand
Makes me want to scream and yell
    speedy dry at hand

Drip on pipes how bad you smell
    is your marking planned
When you dry a sticky jell
    claiming a plot of land

Where you drip from you won't tell
    it stands out like a band
When I find you it will be swell
    dryness will be grand

Show yourself and I will quell
    Harley is my brand
Tighten, torque, and all is well
    ego will be fanned

Guy With The Bug

The guy with the bug in his tooth
Harley rider, to tell the truth
Graduate University of Duluth
Drank a little too much vermouth
Relieved himself off his friends roof
The cops didn't appreciate the spoof
Made him blow, to find out the truth
Now this guy with the bug in his tooth
Graduate University of Duluth
Harley rider, to tell the truth
Did thirty days quite aloof.....

Lovey Dove & Me

Polishing my Harley
Is a labor of love
Usually performed
By my lovey dove

Fixing my Harley
Is just what I do
Because lovey dove
Hasn't a clue

Lovey dove holds tight
As I give it the gas
So she don't fall off
And bruise her cute ass

Riding the Harley
We do as one
Lovey dove and me
Riding for fun

Bad Behavior

Well you've finally done it
You big brave Harley rider
Made a fool out of your self didn't you
In front of all of your friends
You really gave them a show
Camera, action, asshole in motion
Nothing like real time spontaneous stupidity
Thought you had it all under control
When will you ever learn
And look at your beautiful Harley
All dented and busted up
Behavior out of control
Saying that you behaved like a child
Is an insult to children
Glad your kids didn't see that move
Too bad the cops did
Your buddies will ride you for years to come
Embarrassment to the bone...
At least nobody was hurt
A grand or so fixes the bike
A grand or so for the lawyer
No guts, no glory....

Recipe   For   Passion

Take one Harley Davidson
Warm fragrant air
Clear blue sky
No destination
A fair maiden, a fair chance
To finally get in her pants
This Harley injects passion into our souls
A mechanical foreplay
Cerebral masturbation, active imagination
Soft breasts clinging firmly to my back
My spirit soars
Desire, passion, man, woman and machine
The motorcycle god's have provided
Aphrodite work your magic
Time for a passion break
Coasting to stop
In the farmers field by a stream
Mix passionately
Bake in each others arms
Until done.......

1976 Liberty

Liberty 76 you're a classic
    tribute to our past
None of your parts made of plastic
    our pride is unsurpassed

Polishing you makes me spastic
    freedom is amassed
The shine on you sticks like mastic
    Liberty will outlast

AMF years were very drastic
    our numbers growing fast
Harley true bloods made it past it
    dissenters are aghast

Ridden with pride don't have to ask it
    ride Jap and be harassed
Me and HD a team fantastic
    America is's a blast

Emotions

The urge-to-ride meter
Is pegged
A burning desire to ride
Animates my spirit
My Harley beckons
A need that gnaws at my soul
Like an incomplete cure
But when I twist the wick
I'll be gone
Don't bother looking for me
Gone like a ghost
On my way in style
All worldly cares
Blown away with a roar
Only those who ride
The Harley Davidson
Ever experience this
Euphoric state of mind
All others can only
Dream.......

Tidd Bits

My Harley has life
But its heart doesn't beat
Its only alive
With me on the seat

This chariot of mine
Harley by name
Scoots me along
Like heat through a flame

All nonriders
Don't have a clue
Of the ecstasy
That I'm going through

Riding to work
Or just for fun
Riding my Harley
Is number one

Getting Stroked At 60 MPH

My Harley rumbles along rhythmically at 60 mph
The lady of my affections holding on tight
Occasional playful naughty touches
She loves to tease
With hands tethered to the handlebars
I'm helpless to respond
Naughty lady
Now feeling her oats
So she starts feeling her man
My mind races like my cams
Speed, balance and control give way
To passionate thoughts
My gearshift now erect
Over twenty years into this marriage
She's entitled
A mile a minute foreplay
I tap the brakes to feel her breasts strike my back
I want to get off this Harley
And get on her
But I can't let go
And I can't stop here
Ohhhhhh
How she loves to tease

Adrenalin Shot

The adrenalin shot
Self medicated by
The twist of my wrist
The rumble of
My Harley's soul
The front wheel
Lurching for the sky
The reality that
I just might be
Out of control
Staying with it
Bringing it back
Denying fear
Enjoying the rush

There's A Poker Run Today

There's a poker run today
        gonna have some fun
Check the weather and I may
        ride into the sun

See the riders out to play
        party up a ton
The best hand wins the hay
        games have just begun

All my friends and I will stay
        not to be outdone
So much fun makes my day
        old lady's not a nun

Band stopped playing we're on our way
        Harley is number one
Back next year hooray hooray
        All others I will shun

THE REPAIR

I left the wrenches in the dirt
I snatched my helmet from the shelf
I lifted my Harley to it's upright position
I opened the gas cock
I pulled out the choke
I twisted the throttle with anticipation
I turned the key
I pushed the go button
I felt it light up
I heard the confirming roar
I exposed a shit eating grin
I had a moment of satisfaction
I fixed my Harley
I did a great job
I pointed it down the driveway
I let it pull me along the yellow striped path
I experienced karma with my well oiled machine
I may never come back....

Costly Repair

Repairing my Harley
Will cause me some pain
The cost of just parts
An economic drain

The estimate's big
As I knew it would
The noise that it made
It just can't be good

I push it on in
Through the shop door
Mechanic opens it up
Shrapnel hits the floor

They hand me the bill
My heart goes weak
I stutter and stammer
And can't even speak

Girls   Like   You

Girls like you
Give bikers a bad name
A little too loud
Loud and vulgar
You dress like a slut
Too much pasta
On those hips
Too much cleavage
Between those tits
Too much tequila
Through those lips
Too many times
You've been a witch
Too many battles
Gives me the fits
Fat loud and vulgar
But always in my corner
I love you Babe
You're my Harley Bitch

The Antique Harley

The Antique Harley that I
Just restored
Used the best parts
That I could afford
I'm the man
On the Harley
That roared
In the saddle
Up straight I soared
Machine, man and nature
In perfect accord
Finer ride than driving
A Ford
Feelings of eternal bliss
Can't be ignored
Fond memories
My mind will record

Sportster Gas Tank

Sportster gas tank you're so small
    my Harley's very fast
Filled it up-is that all
    never am I last

Two gallons only will quickly fall
    speed is unsurpassed
Hope I make it to the mall
    fast is a blast

You run dry my bike will stall
    the Japs I just passed
May need some help from you-all
    my throttle is very vast

When you're full I really haul
    guess my fate is cast
Faster than a cannon ball
    Speed or empty the contrast

Drifting   Off

Time stands still
As I soar like a meteor
Through deep space
A rhythmic drone from my Harley's
Perfectly balanced pistons
Pushing and pulling fuel and exhaust
Hypnotize my every fiber
A feeling of euphoria overtakes me
As I summon the throttle
The acceleration and the
Deep lean into the corner
Leads me onward down the path
The smile on my face
Expands into moments of tranquility
Smashed by the ringing phone
On my desk
Reality returns
A day dream ends
The work day has just started

The Ride By

The lady turns her head
As I rumble into view
If you smile and wave
I'll blow a kiss to you

Never been on a Harley
Don't know if you like
Come on a ride with me
Give your spirit a spike

Each have private thoughts
As we go our own way
I think I'm smitten
Love to meet you some day

Never to see you again
I lust and I dream
To cover your naked body
With vanilla ice cream

55

Fat Girl

Damn
Woman if you gain
Another pound
I'll need a crane to
Hoist you onto this bike
The strain on my
Drive train
Makes me shudder
Were always last
Going up steep hills
I love you baby
But you just gotta shed
My Harley's taking a beating
Hauling your fat ass
All over town
Please baby
Shed some of that tonnage
I want to be first
Going up those hills

Heaven's Gate

I saw the truck
I heard my belt buckle go
Clink
On the Pearly Gates
I was dead
Hope St. Peter rides a Harley
Glad I was heading north
At the time of the crash
A little momentum in the right direction
Couldn't have hurt
A second ago
I was
Late for work
Late on my car payment
Late on my rent
And my girlfriend was late
Now I'm strolling through Heaven's gate
Hi St. Peter
Hi Jesus
Sister Edward's is gonna shit
When she see's me
I did make it !

The Slamming Of Second Gear

The slamming of second gear
       thrown back in the saddle
Music to this Harley-man's ear
       rider legs a straddle

Passenger ingests a little fear
       teeth tend to rattle
Thrusts us fast away from here
       like stampeding cattle

All Jap bikers to the rear
       taching up the paddle
Wind makes my eyes tear
       like rain in Seattle

The slamming of second gear
       and that I do prattle
Better than an ice cold beer
       soldier's returning from battle

Ready Set Go

Insurance
Good Tires
Gas
Oil
A Harley man
An extraordinary woman
Ignition
The Harley Rumble
Gears
Pistons and cams
Sparks and explosions
Asses in the saddle
Sunglasses on
No destination required
Vroom

Troubles

Waking the neighbors
As he roars home drunk
The little lady
Wants to hide in a trunk

Her Harley man
A sight to behold
Is whispered by neighbors
To be an asshole

A job he can't keep
A yard he can't clean
The lady should leave him
If you know what I mean

Some have it some don't
Not always your call
Don't give into bad times
Just give it your all

Harley Lullaby

Lullaby and good day
Harley friends ride off to play
For a safe ride we all pray
Riding together along the way
Forging friendships here to stay
Great memories are born today
Offering nothing for dismay
When it ends who's to say
All bad wishes kept at bay
Find a place to smoke that jay
Everything will be OK
Let the marbles fall where they may
The unriders all say nay
Harley loyalty will never stray
All these Harleys a great display
The biker image we portray

Tired Old Harley

My valves are ticking
Like the Crock
That ate Captain Hook's
Right hand
My chain
Is slapping
Like the Captain's
Jolly Roger
My shingled tires are thumping
Like Captain Hook's wooden leg
On the poop deck
At midnight
My Harley is tired
And old
It needs
Many pieces of eight
Or a visit from
Peter Pan

Harley Logo Shield And Bar

Harley logo shield and bar
      known to all the world
Number one that you are
      colors are unfurled

Donned by riders near and far
      proudly there are twirled
Place your decal on my car
      the symbolism's hurled

The world knows you're a star
      your name around is swirled
Down the road of waving tar
      creating a new world

Riding you is more than par
      round bars my fingers curled
Riding memories etched a scar
      a biker's life is whirled

Trashed

Gobbling up alcohol
Like it expires tomorrow
Ingesting coke
Smoking dope
In desperate hope
My Harley appears
A blur in the line of bikes
Staggering toward its saddle
A fleeting thought to safety
I should sit and chill
Chemicals abide
A need to ride
Foolish pride
I may not survive
But I will ride
Tomorrow if alive
The same misguided pride
My Harley and I
Am alive

Bad Tire

My rear tire was bad
Gave the scare of my life
Through the wet corner
The bike did jack knife

I let go the throttle
And steered the right way
Caught just in time
Saving my ass and the day

Some riders I fear
Might have panicked and froze
Crashing and burning
God only knows

Ride to the Harley shop
A new tire I say
Money's no object
Live to ride another day

Butcher Mechanic

If your gonna butcher
Butcher good
Get the big hammer
Use the long breaker bar
Connect up that big cutten tip
It ain't hot enough till it melts
Go ahead
Twist it the wrong way
Put the vise grip on that metric nut
Round off that rusty head
Gimme that impact tool
I need a long pipe for more leverage
When it still don't move
Let Bubba Hit it
But please whatever you do
Don't butcher my Harley
It hurts my very soul

Bad Spelling

Eye don't no wye
Aul kar drivers don't
Lok moure carefully when
Maken a you turn
Ore any other tipe of turn
Into ore out of an intersexion
I new that riding my Harley
Was very dangeros so
Eye try to ride very cautiously
Often checkking the heir in my tires
Listening so I can here any daanger
Whearing bright clothing so eye can be scene

Poor Spike got broudsided
He skidded one hundred feat into the swamp
Lucklly the reads were softe and slowed him up
But his bike got scent to the junk pile
Hank went down when a dog tried to byte him
He and da bike was ok
Just a couple of scratcheses
Aul and aul a bykier just has to be caarful
Ore he could wake up dead

Road   Rash

Road rash road rash burns like hell
    my arse skims the deck
Happens so fast it rings my bell
    gonna be a nasty wreck

I got mine when my Harley fell
    hope I don't break my neck
When you get yours you may yell
    glad I mailed insurance check

Top layer of skin turns to jell
    tumbling gracefully like a fleck
Hurts so bad I do tell
    body and bike on different trek

Emergency room that horrible smell
    or my limbs patched every speck
Bottle of Cuddy the pain to quell
    nothing broken what the heck

Shots

There's the shot of Jack Daniels
The shot in the dark
The shot at the target
The shot at passion
The shot for peace
The shot for protection
The shot behind the ear
The shot at the bad guy
The shot in the shorts
The shot heard round the world
Then there's the titty shot
The moon shot
The pussy shot
The blind shot
The missed shot
The long shot
The marksman's shot
The sniper's shot
The first shot
The lethal shot
But there's nothing like
The " Hole Shot " on a tricked out Harley !!!

Race Time

Racing my Harley
My heart goes a twitter
Such roaring power
This magical critter

First off the line
I give it the gas
My racing buddy
Sees only my ass

Redlining my Harley
Is lots of fun
My only threat
The radar gun

So Speeding is great
And winning is cool
Judge fines me dearly
For breaking the rule

Live Harley

I am Harley
But I love my human
I'm man-made, and
A big hairy tattooed human bought me
He made me faster
I love to go fast
Boost me again human
Gimmy that Andrews high lift cam
I want that DeLordo carb
Then I'll be so fast it may scare you
Nobody will be able to catch us
Twist that throttle man
Lean me over in that corner
Change my oil
My valves are clacking human
Adjust my timing, I'm running hot
My name is sportster
Vin 1ZFW4678
I live to ride

Fast Trip

Fuel drenched air
Through my carburetor and valves
Sparks through wires and plugs
Chemicals through my blood stream
Hotter than a lightning bolt
I strangle the throttle for speed
Nailing four big shifts
The journey is on
My Harley thrusts me forward
Like a timeless wave length
Ignoring all speed restrictions
I'll be there before the wind
Minding only the tack's red line
I morph into my magic machine
Becoming one with the moment
Twice the distance takes me half as long
My only regret is that I have arrived
Too fast

Harley   Front   Wheel

Harley front wheel please stay down
      giving it some gas
On my way out of town
      balls are made of brass

Loss of steering makes me frown
      speed limit I do sass
Too much air look like a clown
      mach one methinks I pass

Leaning left so please come round
      this could bruise my ass
Feeling like a king with a crown
      I gained control alas

For my wheelies I am reknowned
      a crash would mean harass
Showing off like a dinner gown
      my legend does amass

Satan Spawned

He was Satan-spawned
And he grew up worse
All his life he bore
That curse
Orphanage refuse
Reform school thug
Prison gangster
With an ugly mug
Joined the angels
And is the one
Who killed the man who stole
His Harley Davidson

The Lesson

Riding my Harley
Minding my own
This kid pulls out
He must be stoned

I hit the brakes hard
My bike goes a-skid
And barely avoid
Hitting this kid

A little road rage
Is good for the soul
A lesson needs to be taught
To that stupid asshole

I roar along-side
And display number one
Cursing his mother
And his first born son

We Wheel

This one's for the boys
Who ride Harley Davidsons
An instinctive desire
To ride the best
Rolling along blacktop trails
Summoning the biker deities
To deliver a grand ride
Feeding our egos to the wind
Weaving to and fro
Within our lanes
Avoiding
Pot holes, bumps, animals and debris
Vigilant always for our lives
Yet carefree in the sun
On our pricey iron steeds
We wheel

Biker's Promenade

Double lanes of leathered souls
Wheel from all corners of the states
Spokes dancing in the sun
Riding till morning blends to night
Engines belching the Harley D concert
Tires stroking pavement
Damn the pigs full speed ahead
Like the cannon ball express
We roar

Destination bike week Daytona
In quest of a happy place
In the sun
Seeking boundless servings
Of enchantment and mayhem
Two weeks to be a
Polar self

When destiny is done
The survivors return
To a common day existence
No longer wayward sons and daughters
Lusting for the
Fantasy express

Just corporal men and women
Trying to cope

Harley Rider Feel So Free

Harley rider feel so free
        mighty as a sword
Makes me want to shout with glee
        blessing from the Lord

Electric start saves my knee
        down the road I roared
Stop at toll to pay the fee
        feeling like I scored

Take me down to the sea
        Harley nature perfect chord
That is where I want to be
        ridden and adored

Park my Harley under that tree
        good karma is restored
Little sportster just you and me
        cannot be ignored

The Judge

The judge rides a Harley
But he don't give a rat's ass about me
He starts spouting some legal jargon
Advising me of my rights
I can't listen
I keep thinking damn yuppie
Spewing legalese like he does a million times day
He rambles on
Twenty grand and new leather don't make you a biker man
The cop ain't here but he's on his way they say
Nailed me doing forty in a thirty
Welcome to Nazi land
The judge declares a ten minute recess
Ten minutes turns into twenty five
Someone go wake the judge
The cop got here ten minutes ago
All rise as the judge strolls in
The man in black
Addresses me
I plead guilty to my assault on society
Pounding his gavel I hear
One hundred thirty-five dollar fine and a
Thirty-five dollar sur charge
I pay the cashier on the way out
I roar away
Hoping to catch the judge on the road some day
There he'll be in my court

Sweetie Pie & I

Sweetie pie and I
Sure love to ride
We giggle and quip
And ride side by side

She has her own Harley
And that's OK too
We ride the day long
Then head home and screw

When the boys ride hard
She jumps on with me
Riding fast and tight
Scares her you see

Sweetie pie and I
Two of a kind
Riding our Harleys
Leaving troubles behind

Harley Davidson

Harley Davidson it's just so motorcycle
First you have all of the different models to choose from
You have the big dresser all the way to
The chopped down drag bikes
You can cruise down the highway at fifty-five
Quiet as a whisper or
You can cruise faster than the Angel Gabriel
And make more noise than the space shuttle

Then there's the clothing
Jackets, boots, gloves, socks, underwear
The list goes on and on
And all of the must have accessories
The Harley wallet, belt buckle, goggles
Pins, decals, coffee mugs, ash trays
The list goes on

Next the Harley traditions
Tee shirt from every dealership you visit
And you always find a Harley dealership
Any time you are in a new state
No Harley rider passes another Harley in distress

Harley Davidson it's just so motorcycle
It's got all of the bells and whistles
But there's nothing like the ride

Demons

The
I- am- cool Demon appears
As I mount my big twin Harley
He is joined by the
I've- got- balls Demon
As well as the Reckless Demon
And I can't ignore the Speed Demon
As he writhes within my skin
Intrepidly I start my engine
The Wheelie Demon rears his ugly head
In submission
I feel my hand strangle the throttle
This man is destined to ride hard today
Just one of those days
Noise, smoke and a front wheel skyward
With the Speed Demon now firmly in control
The excursion is on
Destiny tempts fate
And fate produces
The Law Demon appearing in my mirrors
With his flashing lights
To write the tickets

Harley Four Speed

Harley four speed lacks one gear
      I feel the urge to shift
Take me fast away from here
      my toe I want to lift

Missed that shift I shed a tear
      looking not too swift
One two three oops in my ear
      shift demon set adrift

Found it now at last I cheer
      fifth gear would be a gift
Lift front wheel it's hard to steer
      all riders catch my drift

Grab some throttle cars disappear
      speed limit I just stiffed
Bury the tach for some fear
      but I still want to shift

Friendly Assholes

There's nothing worse than the friendly asshole
My points fell out
The little screw dropped in the dirt when I took off the points cover
And the asshole asks me if I checked the gas

And this guy's waving me on
But he don't see the eighteen wheeler coming
That would squash me like a bug
On a windshield

Then there's the seventy something year old drunk
With breath like Godzilla
And smells like a dumpster at a seafood restaurant
Slurring something about riding an Indian back in 1945

Lets not forget the toothless guy and
His Ritalin deprived brat
Swinging his jacket wildly
His zipper puts a gash in my fender

Yeah they all come out of the woodwork
When you ride a Harley
They all want to be my friend
But I just want to go ride

And be asshole free

Get your own Harley

Birthday Gift

The birthday boy
She ran to greet
With a passionate kiss
You could feel the heat

This Harley rider
And little Ms. Sweet
The most perfect couple
One could ever meet

The man has it all
He owns a small fleet
So many toys
Most men can't compete

So her gift of oral sex
Is a special treat
While sitting on his
Harley's seat

Ride To Work

The sun breaks into the night
Again victorious
It launches a magnificent day
Ripe for exercising my Harley

The warm October morning
Absorbs my spirit
As I wipe the unruly drop of coffee
From my beard

In a trancelike state I march
Helmet in hand
Toward my twenty first century
Iron steed

Hearing the twin pistons roar
I morph into Aladdin
Skillfully gliding through traffic
On my way to work

My Harley brings me peace
And for brief moments
Releases my soul from
Reality

Harley Rider At Night

Windy night feeling like a kite
        sit up straight to gain some height
Excitement engulfs my core
        riding to explore

Harley rider lean to the right
        grab the grips squeeze them tight
Through the corner I soar
        speed limit I ignore

Into the tunnel and see no light
        headlight on into the night
Through the dark I roar
        guardian angel I implore

Smile at me I'm quite a sight
        touch my bike and I will fight
Little Harley I adore
        my loyalty is hard-core

Sunday's Ride

Biker brothers
Plan on a ride
The calls go out
No friend will hide

They set the time
I tell the bride
My Harley friends
Plan Sunday's ride

The sun comes up
And weather's eyed
Harley shirts on
Worn with great pride

We meet at Hess
Then off we glide
My Harley friends
We live to ride

Traffic Jam

Nothings worse than the traffic jam
Any biker knows that
Bumper to bumper inching along
A virtual hell on wheels
The clutch tortures my left hand
Each squeeze is self inflicted pain
If my hand cramps my passenger is in for a wild ride
The big twin is a 180 degree radiator
Vibrating between my thighs
Roasting my legs
Car drivers don't have a clue of the hell
That this Harley rider is going through
The mid-day sun beats on my black helmet
Baking my head like an Idaho potato
The blacktop road becomes a cookie sheet
Baking souls of my feet as I yearn to ride
The smell of diesel exhaust
Settles heavily in my lungs
I can't see a thing except the graffiti
On the back of the big rig in front of me
If hell is hotter than this
I'm gonna change my way's
If it don't clear in five more minutes
This rider is rolling down the shoulder

Harley Helmet

Harley helmet save my head
      when the crash calls
Keep me conscious and not dead
      as my Harley falls

Wishing I was home in bed
      now my engine stalls
Soon I'll be seeing red
      handlebars whack my balls

Pavement and I have just been wed
      tumbling my body sprawls
Layers of skin will soon be shed
      slow motion like southern drawls

Mr. Fate needs to be fed
      in pain the time crawls
To the hospital I'll be led
      wheel me down the halls

Pissed

Her Harley man
Got her pissed
She saw the girl
That he just kissed

Her short temper
Won't desist
The little slut
Will meet her fist

Life has it's rules
She won't be dissed
The little slut
Just met her fist

Her Harley man
Will insist
It nothing
Please don't be pissed

Road Rage Lug Nut

Riding my Harley five over the limit
The car appears in my mirrors
Now he's right on my tail light
A courteous back off wave I signal
For safety with my left hand
It produces a middle finger
From the offending driver
Then he inches closer
Turning I look straight into his face
I angrily return the gesture
And another back off wave
He inches closer and leans on his horn
Now he's threatening my life
Right hand in jacket pocket finds
The road rage lug nut
With a quick flip of the wrist over the shoulder
The back off missile is launched
The screeching brakes reports that it found it's mark
Wonder how much the windshield costs for that big Mercedes
Wonder if he learned a lesson
It's dangerous to tailgate this biker

Traffic   Fairy

Traffic fairy hexed my lane
      tires lose their grip
Reality is the driving rain
      o'er the bars I do the flip

Downpour in northern Maine
      riding Harley is very hip
Direct result of monetary gain
      maturity and biking is a quip

Kissing the ground causes pain
      clothing starts to rip
In my pants appears a stain
      IV they'll start a drip

This is no time to be vain
      happened in a zip
Walking forever requires a cane
      mobility fate did strip

I Got She Got

I got the Harley
She got the house
The judge has no spine
And the balls of a mouse

I got the truck
She got the Vette
The judge has no spine
He'll get his yet

She got the dog
I got shit
The judge has no spine
I want to spit

She got the big screen
I got the remote
The judge has no spine
It all gets my goat

The Skid Mark

The big shift
That he slammed
Launched his
Front wheel skyward
Planting a smile
On his face
And glory to his soul
But the raw power
And intense acceleration
Left a skid mark
In his girlfriend's
Knickers
Sometimes
Her Harley riding man
Rides too hard
So she tries real hard
To suppress
Her fear
And she hangs on tight

Gear Gremlin Grungy Grinch

Gear Gremlin grungy Grinch
      demon leave my bike
Giving Harley's engine a flinch
      trouble I don't like

Going to repair shop that's a cinch
      Gremlin take a hike
Got to give the gears a clinch
      mechanics name is Mike

Gripping loose gears just a sminch
      then hammer like a spike
Getting tighter just one more inch
      now all gears aligned alike

Gear Gremlin grungy Grinch
      demon left my bike
Got wallet scar felt the pinch
      glad I'm not on strike

Downpour

The long ride home starts at 1700
A standard Navy clock ticks 0815
It's raining, not just raining
A downpour, a torrent of rain and wind
Hammering the office windows

My Harley sits tightly covered
Just outside the Main Gate
Motorcycles aren't allowed
On this Submarine Base, Groton, Ct.
Forecast is heavy rain and wind all day
Forecast is a very wet ride home tonight
The usual two hour trip home, Carmel, NY
Will probably turn into a very soggy
Three hours or more
My workday is haunted by flashbacks
Of previous rides home in the rain

That sinking feeling I get in my gut
As my Harley hydroplanes through a puddle
Raindrops explode on my face and skin
Like small atomic bombs, pummeling my flesh
Stopping just after the toll booth
To drain the water out of my boots
Eighteen wheelers that combine vortices and wind
Into a blinding spray, turning my limited vision
Into a scary, watery blur

1700 finds me marching toward my Harley
Weary with thoughts of the adventure at hand
I forge on gritting my teeth, as the rain pounds, I light the fire
And this Submarine sailor heads home
With attitude!

Loose   Chain

My Harley has a loose chain
    can't you hear the slap
Power shifts caused the strain
    shifting with that snap

Flapping chain gives sprocket pain
    rear sprocket turns to scrap
My wallet has just been slain
    big money that's no crap

Extra cash went down the drain
    I'm an unlucky chap
Gotta fix it to my disdain
    old lady's mouth a flap

My Harley helps to keep me sane
    I won't ride a Jap
Proudly riding down the lane
    I'll call that a wrap

Rumble Withdrawal

It's a temporary insanity
Usually afflicting us cold winter dwellers
Hits hardest 'bout February
The rumble of Harley pipes cruising by the door
Has long been replaced by the drone of the midnight snowplow Three feet of
frozen snow buries the path to the shed
That snugly packages my Road King
It's as if all Harleys went extinct
Haven't heard one for months now
There is an emptiness of the soul
Like some appendage has been plucked from my body Rumble withdrawal
It gets bad
You know the symptoms
I've been getting them over 42 years now
Trouble sleeping, nightmares of sterility
Irritable, possible nausea, and diarrhea
Pretty serious shit, pun intended
The only cure is at least two months away
Watching the motorcycle races on TV can add a rash
If you're really sensitive
Sometimes when I have a very bad day
I dream of ways that I could drive my Harley in the living room
I told you it gets bad
All in due time the snow melts
Spring kicks winter's ass
I throw my leg over my custom leather seat
Push that little black button
Hear that sweet rumble, then
Instant cure
No therapy necessary
And no scar

Early Morning Ride

The cool wind slaps my face
       Harley rumbles in my ear
Twisted throttle ups the pace
       heart erupts into a cheer

All cares gone without a trace
       euphoria in abundance here
Just one union with time and space
       with each rhythmic shifting gear

Harley moments to embrace
       vivid memories very clear
Memories made will never erase
       the morning sun does appear

Far away from the rat race
       feeling like a pioneer
Gliding toward a special place
       heading to a new frontier

Made in the USA
Columbia, SC
02 December 2018